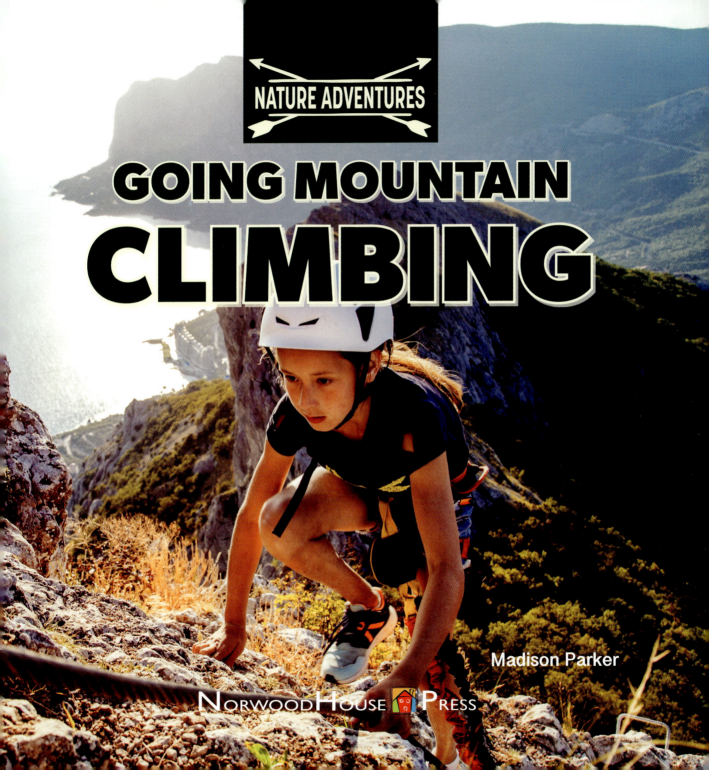

Cataloging-in-Publication Data

Names: Parker, Madison.
Title: Going mountain climbing / Madison Parker.
Description: Buffalo, NY : Norwood House Press, 2026. | Series: Nature adventures | Includes glossary and index.
Identifiers: ISBN 9781978574717 (pbk.) | ISBN 9781978574724 (library bound) | ISBN 9781978574731 (ebook)
Subjects: LCSH: Mountaineering--Juvenile literature. | Rock climbing--Juvenile literature.
Classification: LCC GV200.P375 2026 | DDC 796.522--dc23

Published in 2026 by
Norwood House Press
2544 Clinton Street
Buffalo, NY 14224

Copyright © 2026 Norwood House Press
Designer: Rhea Magaro
Editor: Kim Thompson

Photo credits: Cover, p. 1, 6 Alexandra Golubtsova/Shutterstock.com; p. 5 Photobac/Shutterstock.com; p. 7 everst/Shutterstock.com; p. 9 JJ pixs/Shutterstock.com; p. 10 Alex Brylov/Shutterstock.com; pp. 11, 13 Soloviova Liudmyla/Shutterstock.com; pp. 12, 16 Sergey Novikov/Shutterstock.com; pp. 14, 15 zhukovvvlad/Shutterstock.com; p. 17 honzik7/Shutterstock.com; p. 18 Anna Nahabed/Shutterstock.com; p. 19 PiXel Perfect PiX/Shutterstock.com; p. 21 Melinda J Johnson/Shutterstock.com;

All rights reserved. No part of this book may be reproduced in any form without permission in writing from the publisher, except by a reviewer.

Printed in the United States of America

Some of the images in this book illustrate individuals who are models. The depictions do not imply actual situations or events.

CPSIA compliance information: Batch #CSNHP26: For further information contact Norwood House Press at 1-800-237-9932.

TABLE OF CONTENTS

What Is Mountain Climbing?..4

Mountain Climbing Supplies..8

Mountain Climbing Safety..14

Where to Go Mountain Climbing..18

Glossary..22

Thinking Questions..23

Index...24

About the Author..24

WHAT IS MOUNTAIN CLIMBING?

Let's go mountain climbing! Mountain climbing is a fun outdoor activity.

Mountain climbing is when people climb up to mountain **peaks**. Many people like to have mountain climbing adventures.

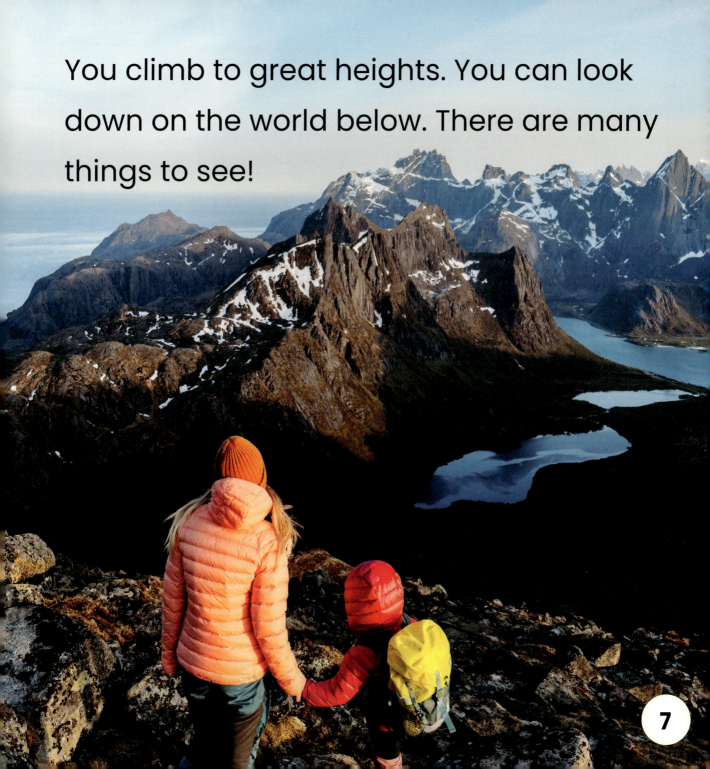

You climb to great heights. You can look down on the world below. There are many things to see!

MOUNTAIN CLIMBING SUPPLIES

You need a lot of gear for mountain climbing. Boots give your ankles extra support. **Crampons** help you grip rocks and ice.

A helmet protects you if you hit your head. It protects you from falling **debris**.

A climbing rope catches you if you fall. It must be very strong. It must **absorb** the energy of your fall.

A **belay** system connects the climber to a person at the base of the mountain who is called a belayer. The climber and the belayer wear belay devices. The rope goes between them.

The belay device and rope are connected through a **harness**. Both the climber and the belayer wear a harness.

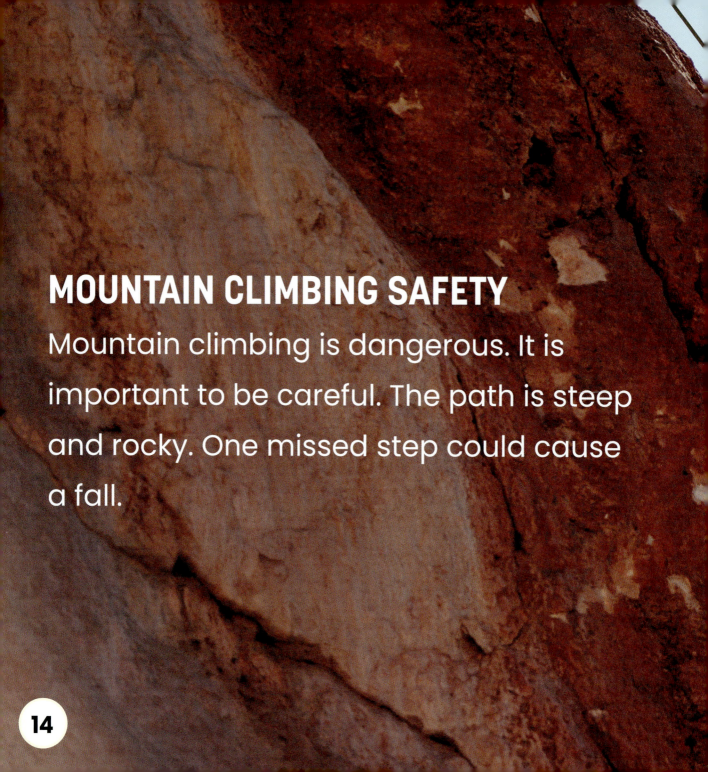

MOUNTAIN CLIMBING SAFETY

Mountain climbing is dangerous. It is important to be careful. The path is steep and rocky. One missed step could cause a fall.

Climbers must hold tight to the climbing rope. They must communicate with the belayer.

Mountain climbers should Leave No **Trace** (LNT). That means you should not leave trash or anything else behind.

Leave the **wilderness** better than you found it. This protects **wildlife**.

17

WHERE TO GO MOUNTAIN CLIMBING

There are many good places for mountain climbing. You do not have to climb real mountains. You can climb indoor climbing walls.

It is important to read any **regulations** before you go.

You can visit your state's park website to find mountain climbing spots near you. Mountain climbing helps you explore the great outdoors!

Glossary

absorb (ab-ZORB): to soak up

belay (bi-LAY): a rope system that connects the climbing rope to the climber and to a person on the ground

crampons (KRAM-pahnz): metal spikes that attach to boots to help climbers grip icy or rocky surfaces

debris (duh-BRIS): small pieces of rock or dirt that can fall while climbing

harness (HAHR-nis): a belt that keeps climbers attached to the climbing rope

peaks (peeks): the highest points of mountains; mountaintops

regulations (reg-yuh-LAY-shuhnz): rules you need to follow

trace (trays): a sign that someone has been in a place; evidence

wilderness (WIL-dur-nis): wild land where no people live

wildlife (WILDE-life): wild animals living in their natural environment

Thinking Questions

1. What is mountain climbing?

2. Why is wearing a helmet important when mountain climbing?

3. How does using a climbing rope help a climber?

4. Who is a belayer?

5. Where can you go mountain climbing?

Index

belay 12, 13, 15

boots 8

climbing rope 11–13, 15

crampons 8

fall 11, 14

harness 13

helmet 10

indoor 18

mountains 6, 12, 18

wildlife 17

About the Author

Madison Parker spent her childhood in the city of Chicago, Illinois. A farm girl at heart, today she lives in Wisconsin with her husband and four children on a small farm with cows, goats, chickens, and two miniature horses named Harley and David. Her favorite dessert is vanilla frozen custard with rainbow sprinkles, even in the winter.